KIDS ON EARTH

Wildlife Adventures – Explore The World
Sun Bear - Cambodia

Sensei Paul David

COPYRIGHT PAGE

Kids On Earth: Wildlife Adventures - Explore The World

Sun Bear - Cambodia

by Sensei Paul David,

Copyright © 2023.

All rights reserved.

978-1-77848-209-0 KoE_WildLife_Amazon_PaperbackBook_cambodia_sun bear

978-1-77848-208-3 KoE_WildLife_Amazon_eBook_cambodia_sun bear

978-1-77848-434-6 KoE_Wildlife_Ingram_PaperbackBook_SunBear Paperback

This book is not authorized for free distribution copying.

www.senseipublishing.com

@senseipublishing
#senseipublishing

Synopsis

This book explores 30 unique and fun facts about sun bears in Cambodia. It covers topics such as their size, diet, behavior, habitat, and more. It also discusses the important role sun bears play in the local culture and ecology, and the threats they face from habitat loss and poaching. Finally, it encourages readers to help protect and conserve sun bears for future generations.

Get Our FREE Books Now!

kidsonearth.life

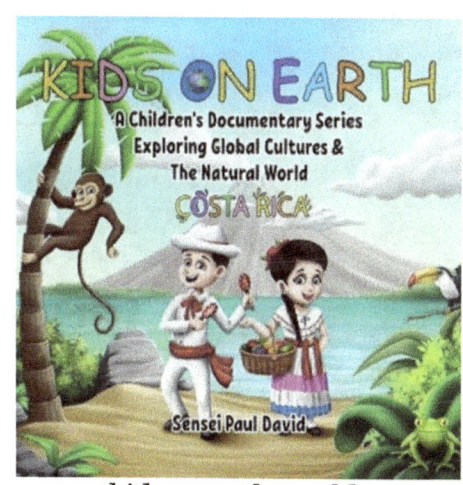

kidsonearth.world

Click Below for Another Book In Each Series

senseipublishing.com/KoE_SERIES

senseipublishing.com/KoE_Wildlife_SERIES

KoE En Español

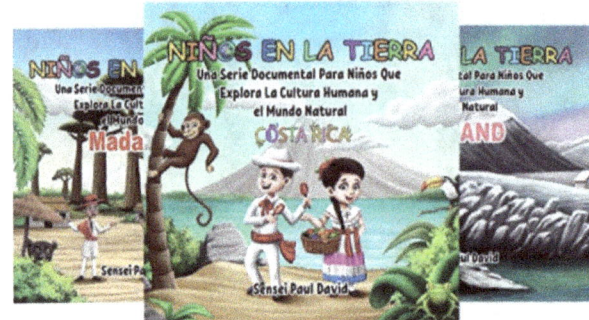

senseipublishing.com/KoE_SERIES_SPANISH

www.senseipublishing.com

Join Our Publishing Journey!

If you would like to receive FUTURE FREE BOOKS and get to know us better, please click www.senseipublishing.com and join our newsletter by entering your email address in the pop-up box.

Follow Our Blog: senseipauldavid.ca

Follow/Like/Subscribe: Facebook, Instagram, YouTube: @senseipublishing

Scan the QR Code with your phone or tablet to follow us on social media:

Like / Subscribe / Follow

Introduction

Welcome to the Sun Bear in Cambodia! Sun Bears are one of the most unique and fascinating animals in the world. They are found in the tropical rainforests of Southeast Asia and are the smallest species of bear. In Cambodia, sun bears play an important role in the local culture and ecosystem. In this book, we will explore the fascinating facts about sun bears in Cambodia so that readers can learn more about this species' fascinating behavior, habitat, and more!

Sun Bears can weigh up to 100 pounds.

Sun Bears are the smallest species of bear.

Sun Bears are omnivores, meaning they eat both plants and animals.

Sun Bears are found in the tropical rainforests of Southeast Asia, including Cambodia.

Sun Bears are active during the day, sleeping in trees at night.

Sun Bears have short, curved claws that help them climb trees.

Sun Bears have a long tongue that helps them eat honey and insects.

Sun Bears are excellent hunters and can catch small prey with their long claws.

Sun Bears are very vocal and have a variety of vocalizations from huffs and grunts to roars.

Sun Bears are solitary animals and usually only come together for mating.

Sun Bears have a white V-shaped marking on their chest.

Sun Bears are threatened by habitat loss and poaching.

Sun Bears are very curious and intelligent animals.

Sun Bears are often seen exchanging "gifts" with one another.

Sun Bears use their long tongues to extract honey from tree trunks.

Sun Bears are social animals and live in groups in the wild.

Sun Bears are excellent swimmers and can hold their breath for up to five minutes.

Sun Bears use their sharp claws to dig for food.

Sun Bears are very protective of their young and will do anything to defend them.

Sun Bears have poor eyesight but an excellent sense of smell.

Sun Bears are active during the day and sleep in trees at night.

Sun Bears are known to be quite playful and can often be seen playing with one another.

Sun Bears can live up to 25 years in the wild.

Sun Bears are very territorial and will mark their territory with urine and claw marks.

Sun Bears are excellent climbers and can climb up to 100 feet in a single jump.

Sun Bears are known to hoard food and can store up to 100 pounds of food in their dens.

Sun Bears can run up to 30 miles per hour.

Sun Bears have a thick coat of fur that helps them keep cool in hot climates.

Sun Bears are expert tree-dwellers and can sleep in the same tree for weeks at a time.

Sun Bears are important to the Cambodian ecosystem and local culture.

Conclusion

Sun Bears in Cambodia are truly incredible animals. They are small, yet powerful, and play an important role in the local culture and ecosystem. Sun Bears are threatened by habitat loss and poaching, but they are also incredibly intelligent, curious, and social animals. We hope that this book has given readers an insight into the fascinating world of sun bears in Cambodia, and that they can help to protect and conserve this species for future generations.

Thank you for reading this book!

If you found this book helpful, I would be grateful if you would **post an honest review on Amazon** so this book can reach other supportive readers like you!

All you need to do is digitally flip to the back and leave your review. Or visit amazon.com/author/senseipauldavid click the correct book cover and click on the blue link next to the yellow stars that say, "customer reviews."

As always...

It's a great day to be alive!

Share Our FREE eBooks Now!

kidsonearth.life

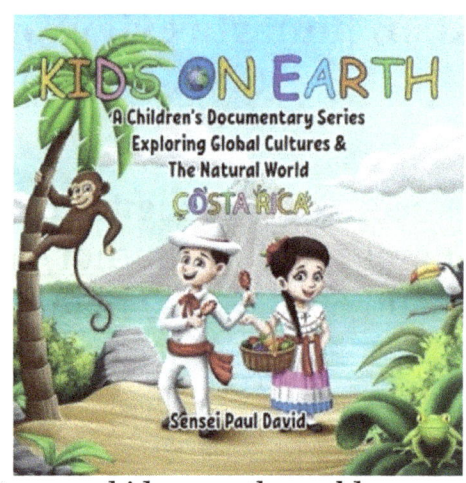

kidsonearth.world

Click Below for Another Book In Each Series

senseipublishing.com/KoE_SERIES

senseipublishing.com/KoE_Wildlife_SERIES

KoE En Español

senseipublishing.com/KoE_SERIES_SPANISH

www.senseipublishing.com

www.senseipublishing.com

@senseipublishing
#senseipublishing

Check out our **recommendations** for other books for adults & kids plus other great resources by visiting
www.senseipublishing.com/resources/

Join Our Publishing Journey!

If you would like to receive FREE BOOKS and special offers, please visit www.senseipublishing.com and join our newsletter by entering your email address in the pop-up box

Follow Our Engaging Blog NOW!
senseipauldavid.ca

Get Our FREE Books Today!

Click & Share the Links Below

FREE Kids Books

lifeofbailey.senseipublishing.com

kidsonearth.senseipublishing.com

FREE Self-Development Book

senseiselfdevelopment.senseipublishing.com

FREE BONUS!!!
Experience Over 25 FREE Engaging Guided Meditations!

Prized Skills & Practices for Adults & Kids. Help Restore Deep Sleep, Lower Stress, Improve Posture, Navigate Uncertainty & More.

Download the Free Insight Timer App and click the link below:
http://insig.ht/sensei_paul

About Sensei Publishing

Sensei Publishing commits itself to helping people of all ages transform into better versions of themselves by providing high-quality and research-based self-development books with an emphasis on mental health and guided meditations. Sensei Publishing offers well-written e-books, audiobooks, paperbacks, and online courses that simplify complicated but practical topics in line with its mission to inspire people toward positive transformation.

It's a great day to be alive!

About the Author

I create simple & transformative eBooks & Guided Meditations for Adults & Children proven to help navigate uncertainty, solve niche problems & bring families closer together.

I'm a former finance project manager, private pilot, jiu-jitsu instructor, musician & former University of Toronto Fitness Trainer. I prefer a science-based approach to focus on these & other areas in my life to stay humble & hungry to evolve. I hope you enjoy my work and I'd love to hear your feedback.

- It's a great day to be alive!
Sensei Paul David

Scan & Follow/Like/Subscribe: Facebook, Instagram, YouTube: @senseipublishing

Scan using your phone/iPad camera for Social Media
Visit us at www.senseipublishing.com and sign up for our newsletter to learn more about our exciting books and to experience our FREE Guided Meditations for Kids & Adults.

www.ingramcontent.com/pod-product-compliance
Lightning Source LLC
Chambersburg PA
CBHW080617110526
44587CB00040BB/3732